Sloightly on
th' Huh !

D1643380

Keep a-trogu
gad !.

21·05·11

Sloightly on th' Huh!

An affectionate look at the Suffolk dialect

Charlie Haylock

with illustrations by Richard Scollins
and Barrie Appleby

COUNTRYSIDE BOOKS
NEWBURY BERKSHIRE

First published 2004
© Charlie Haylock, 2004

COUNTRYSIDE BOOKS
3 Catherine Road
Newbury, Berkshire

To view our complete range of books,
please visit us at
www.countrysidebooks.co.uk

ISBN 1 85306 877 2

For David, Simon and William

Designed by Peter Davies, Nautilus Design
Produced through MRM Associates Ltd., Reading
Typeset by Techniset Typesetters, Newton-le-Willows
Printed by Woolnough Bookbinding Ltd., Irthlingborough

CONTENTS

ACKNOWLEDGEMENTS

I would like to thank the following people, organisations, pubs and clubs, societies, associations and companies, in helping me in my research for this book on the Suffolk dialect. Without their input, this book would never have been written.

Gordon Alecock
Joyce Alecock
David Allen
Barrie Appleby
BBC Radio Suffolk
Cliff and Penny Baker
Brandon Heritage
Bulmer Brick Works
Peter Carter
Kay Clarke
Gavin Downes
Eastbridge Eel's Foot
Edwardstone White Horse
Bill Haylock
Ray and Cecil Hills
Holbrook Swan
Holbrook Steel Quoits Club
Mr R. Hubbard

Ashley Hunt
Kentwell Hall
Laxfield Low House
Long Melford Folk Club
Patrick Lovell
Low House Albion Band
    (and all who sail in her)
Tony Minter
F. E. Neaves & Son
Hycies Parker
Yvonne and Terry Pettit
Ryes School
Margaret Short
Les Snell
Suffolk Record Office
Suffolk Steel Quoits Association
Westley Club
Eileen and Vonny Whymark

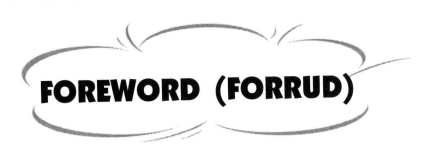

FOREWORD (FORRUD)

'**F**orruds bor! Not arssl'ns' ...... 'Howd yew haard bor!' ...... 'Taint ser bit loikely' ...... 'Sloightly on th' huh!' ...... 'Moind how yew goo cumm'n baack' ...... 'Th' best paart a' fair few' ...... 'Dew yew keep a' throsh'n bor!' ...... ''At duzzy fuel maykes a hellava dullor' ...... 'A good toidlee sum' ...... 'Cood blaarst! 'At's hooly dungy!' ...... 'Shess bor!' ...... ''At's rain'n fairly oover Will's muther's!'

What does it all mean? Why write a book on the Suffolk dialect? Why me?

Suffolk is generally accepted, by historians and academics alike, as being the first page of English history. It's where the English (the Angles) first settled and gave England, English and East Anglia their names. It is where the Angles and Saxons first mixed and formed the basis for our rich language – Anglo-Saxon was on the scene ... in Suffolk.

So, Suffolk is where the English language began and by simple deduction, Suffolk is the oldest English dialect. Reason enough, therefore, to write a book on this historic tongue.

Suffolk is a complete mix of all our uninvited guests, from the Romans to the Normans, plus those that were invited, like the Dutch. Only in Suffolk, do you find this particular rich mix, at the same time maintaining a strong Anglo-Saxon foundation; although north Essex and Norfolk are very similar.

The countryside is a gently rolling agricultural scene that does not suddenly change and go anywhere else, very much like the Suffolkers themselves. However, Lowestoft is the most easterly point of the British Isles, and Suffolk takes the brunt of the North Sea, with villages like Slaughden and Dunwich almost being washed away; and it has hardened to it, just like its people. So under that easy going manner and that laid back approach, you will find a steely determination and doggedness.

From Anglo-Saxon times to medieval times, Suffolk was the most densely populated and richest county. The wool trade was centred there in Tudor times, and even today, throughout Suffolk, thousands of Tudor-framed merchant houses and buildings are still standing, and have become world famous landmarks. Some are now in the care of the National Trust, some are open to the public and some remain as they were. So, nearly every village in the county has its large manor or big hall.

SLOIGHTLY ON TH' HUH!

Tudor Kentwell Hall c.1900

Suffolk also has a lengthy history with the sea and, in the past, the fishing industry has been very important to Suffolk, with Lowerst'ff being the most famous fishing town. Today, the fishing industry is struggling to survive, and some modern Suffolk folk songs depict its demise. It's still alive, though ... just.

The far west of the county, just like Ireland, is full of 'little people'. If you are five feet ten inches tall, walking through Newmarket on a busy day, you are a giant. The place is full of tiny jockeys and stable lads. The horse racing industry is big in west Suffolk, with many training grounds, stables and world famous Tattersalls.

This complete mix between the various European people who have settled, and the fishing, agricultural and associated industries, has led to a unique dialect, which lends itself to the Suffolk humour and complements it thoroughly.

Up till about fifty years ago, East Anglia was very insular; it was that large lump on the side of England. No one passed through to get somewhere else. You actually had to visit the place. This meant the dialect was largely unspoiled by

8

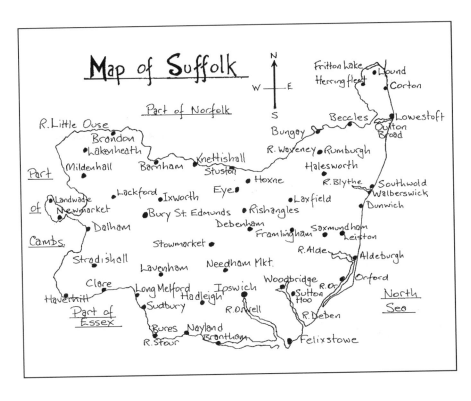

outside influences, especially inland, away from the coast and the limited number of resorts.

However, Suffolk was invaded again, along its southern border, with the building of large housing estates in Great Cornard and Haverhill. A big influx from London and those Saxons again from south Essex swept in. These people have immigrated by their thousands and have created a new south Suffolk dialect. The London/Suffolk mix has led to an Australian-type sound and is often mistaken for one by people from outside the area. This invasion is now spreading to other parts of Suffolk.

Generally, with films, TV, videos, radio, CDs, travel, movement of labour, so-called education and a host more influences, the English dialects appear to be changing into accents, which are changing into brogues, which are changing into lilts, which are changing into a sameness. Fortunately there are still enough people living to keep the Suffolk dialect alive for a while longer yet. Hopefully this book will have a lasting effect and record the Suffolk tongue for ever, and encourage more Suffolkers to hold on to their unique and historic dialect.

FOREWORD (FORRUD)

I was brought up in a Suffolk family, and in the evenings, with no television, would listen to tales and yarns from my parents and grandparents, depicting the good times and the hardships of Suffolk life. These tales and yarns would be steeped in Suffolk traditions and sometimes would make comment on the changes taking place throughout their lifetimes, some for the better and some for the 'wusser'. I heard how my grandfather, Old Bill Haylock, in his own lifetime saw the first motorbike and motor car drive through the villages of Hartest and Stanstead, and yet sat up all night in 1969 and watched a man land on the moon. He lived till he was 90 years old, and had a wealth of knowledge and experience, which spilled over into his yarns. I heard how my father and uncle, Tubal and Arthur, flooded all the lowlands of Snape when opening up the sluice gates to play Pooh sticks. I heard how these two brothers would push their invalid mother, in a 'grit' old wheelchair, from Snape to Aldeburgh and back, every other Sunday. But, when they came to the hill going down into Aldeburgh, they would run and push like mad, till it went so fast they had to hang on the back – just to give the old gal a thrill.

I heard all manner of tales and yarns about childhood, work in traditional trades, poaching, village schools, the family and many many more. Some were humorous, some were sad and seldom told, all were true, some were exaggerated, nothing was written down, all word of mouth.

With this background it's no wonder that I started writing my own brand of amusing Suffolk mardles and monologues, calling on the richness of my family's story telling and yarn spinning, together with my own observation of life. My CD, *That's just cost you a beer*, has been highly successful in Suffolk, and has been bought by Suffolk County Council for their libraries and their archives for the Suffolk voice spoken in verse. I have written for the *East Anglian Daily Times* in their monthly 'Suffolk' magazine on the local dialect and appeared several times on Radio Suffolk on the same subject.

Years ago, the schools would try and teach us Standard English, and try and lose the dialects; but now, in a more enlightened age, I have been employed to visit schools and lecture to English students on the history of the English language and, in particular, the history of the Suffolk dialect . . . WE MUST NEVER LOSE IT!

Charlie Haylock

Courtesy of the Westley Club

CHAPTER 1

Suffolk Hoomer

Suffolk humour (hoomer) is exceedingly funny to the Suffolker, but is often misunderstood by *furreners* and, indeed, is regularly missed altogether.

Joke telling is not so prevalent in Suffolk as in other areas. Humour here tends to be inspired by circumstances; it is paradoxical, literal, and often delivered in the form of a one-liner uttered with a deadpan expression. The punchline is normally a piece of uncomplicated logic, which in itself is rare outside Suffolk, and is quite brilliant and clever; there is always a twist.

Story-telling is common, and is usually accompanied with little asides and diversions that can make the telling hilariously funny.

The slowness of Suffolk speech, with its sing-song lilt, has meant that Suffolkers have been made fun of for many, many years by them there *furreners*. But, what them there *furreners* don't realize is that the Suffolkers know what's going on, and take it in their stride: with their deadpan faces and unique wit and humour, they will get their own back, and in such a way that the recipient is quite unaware. Examples of this type of humour, and the rest, will be found in the next few pages.

The Furrener and the Budget

One autumn evening in a Suffolk pub, five locals – Darkie Deakons, Charlie Whymonger, Doody Parkes, and Tubal and Tinny Alecock – sat close together in their corner, three by the fire and two next to the bar on the far side, opposite the door. No one else was in the public bar. A stranger came in, and instead of going to the vacant part of the bar, nearer the door, he entered the inner sanctum and stood between the two brothers sitting at the bar. He didn't say 'Good evening', 'Hello', or anything – he just totally ignored them.

After a quiet lull in proceedings as the five locals eyed the stranger up and down, Darkie Deakons (so called because of his jet black hair and moustache, and his constant five o'clock shadow) said, 'Cort enny rabb'ts laytlee, Chaarlie?' The coded signal was given; the fun was about to begin.

The stranger ordered a light and bitter, turned to the locals present, and said, 'Bleedin' Chancellor!'

Darkie: Wot yew say?

Stranger: Bleedin' Chancellor!

Darkie: Nuth'n wrong wi' th' Chanceler; wee loike 'm heeya.

Charlie: 'At's roight.

Doody: 'At's a fact, bor.

Stranger: He's put the bleedin' price of petrol up.

Darkie: Oi bet yew're from town, Lunn'n, Oi reck'n.

Stranger: Yeah. How do you know?

Darkie: 'Cos yew townies never lern. Oi've bin goo'n t' 'iss 'ere garridge fer fifteen year, and he charges me th' sayme fer petr'l then as he do now.

Charlie: 'At's roight.

Doody: 'At's a fact, bor.

Stranger: How come?

Darkie: Well, th' Chanceler hev put th' proice a gallons up, 'n' yew buggers never lern: yew townies still goo 'n' aarst fer four gall'ns, foive gall'ns, whatever. But we aarst for foive pounds' worth. He charged uss foive pound 'en 'n' he chaarge uss foive pounds now.

Charlie: 'At's roight.

Doody: 'At's a fact, bor.

Stranger: But you don't get as much petrol!

Darkie: Wot dew yew mean? He don't put four pound ten shill'ns in 'n' aarst fer a foiver. He put in foive pounds 'n' he charges foive pounds. Moind yew, he don't put in foive pounds ten shill'ns 'n' charge a foiver. Just the foiver's worth.

Stranger: But you don't get as much petrol!

Darkie: See ... yew buggers never lern. In fact Oi git more fer moy munny. In 'at toime th' Chanceler hev devalued the pound twoice, soo Oi git more fer me munny. Yew duzzy fuel! Caarn't yew see 'at?

Charlie: 'At's roight.

Doody: 'At's a fact, bor.

Stranger: But you don't get as much <u>PETROL!</u>

Tubal: 'At's noo good, Daarkie, 'ay never lern.

Tinny: He jest doont see ut, do he? Duzzy owd fuel.

The exasperated stranger is hurrying his pint to go.

Darkie: Moind yew, Chaarlie, Oi doon't appear t' git ser menny moiles t' th' gall'n ai wot Oi used to!

Tubal: More doont Oi!

Tinny: Me neether.

Charlie: 'At's roight.

Doody: 'At's a fact bor!

The stranger finished his pint, looked at the serious-looking gathering in total and utter disbelief, and left very quickly. Suddenly, seven broad grins appeared, on the faces of the five locals, the landlord – and you, having just read this true story. But, if the stranger had been polite in the first place and followed protocol, this story would never have happened . . . or would it?

This cartoon was inspired by the late Ray and Cecil Hills of Edwarstone after the 1987 hurricane

CHAPTER 2

Suffolk Place-Names

The names of villages and towns in Suffolk demonstrate the cosmopolitan nature of its history, although the vast majority are nevertheless Anglo-Saxon in origin.

As in the other areas of England that came under Anglo-Saxon control, many Suffolk place-names are actually made up of the personal name of a local Anglo-Saxon chieftain or leader, plus the type of settlement added at the end. Places ending in ton (*tūn*) usually means a 'farmstead' or 'enclosure' (e.g. Stuston, in which the personal name is *Stūt*); ham (*hām*) 'homestead', 'hamlet' or 'manor' (e.g. Saxmundham, formed with the personal name *Seaxmund*); field (*feld*) is 'open land' (e.g. Sternfield, with *Sterne*), or leigh or ley (*lēah*) 'woodland clearing' (e.g. Eleigh, with *Illa*; Gazeley, from *Gægi*; Hemley from *Helma*; and Otley, with the personal name *Otta*). While *ing* in the middle or at the end of a place-name usually means the 'family' or 'people', belonging to the chieftain (e.g. Cretingham, Framlingham and Nedging Tye). Many small hamlets and villages in Suffolk end with the suffix *tye*. This is a dialect word denoting a large common pasture and is more or less confined to Suffolk, where it is quite common (e.g. Bower House Tye, Cornard Tye, Dorking Tye, Honey Tye, Kersey Tye, Stoke Tye, to name but a few); only a very few examples are found outside the county.

Place names ending in -ey, -ay, or -eye tend to denote land surrounded by water, or a dry area of higher land in a marsh or bog. Again, this element is sometimes associated with a personal name, (e.g. Bungay and Lindsey). However, Eye has no chief's name at all. Could it be that Eye was a commune or common land, and became the first village to be in the 'public eye'?! I think not ... just an island in the middle of extensive marshland. The prefix *Kers* in Kersey, either refers to an assembly place (assembly island) or watercress (cress island) – the experts do not yet see 'ey' to 'ey'. Nayland is a shortened version of 'atten-ay-land'.

Bury St Edmunds is so called, because it was an Anglo-Saxon *burh* 'fort', 'stronghold'. The dedication is to Edmund, a 9th century king of East Anglia, who was canonized, according to legend, because he would not share his Christian

kingdom with invading Danes, who then promptly tied him to a tree and filled him with arrows. The diocese is known as St Edmundsbury, and this technically would be more correct.

Ipswich, is an Anglo-Saxon *wīc* 'port' or 'trading place' associated with a man called *Gip*, and recorded in Domesday Book (1086) as *Gipeswic*. The Angle and Saxon variants in pronunciation are uniquely preserved in Ipswich (the softened *g* of the Angles, pronounced *y* – *Yipeswic*, having eventually become lost), while the Saxon hard *g* is retained in names such as Gippeswick and the River Gipping.

There are, of course, many other Anglo-Saxon place-names, too numerous to list, but some odd ones are worth mentioning. Ashbocking ('place at the ash trees' belonging to the Bocking family, Culpho (Cuthwulf's ridge), Herringfleet ('creek or stream of the family or followers of Herela'), Knodishall-cum-Buxloe (Cnott's shelter or nook of land near a deer's burial ground), Orford (possibly 'the ford near the shore'; the river name, Ore, is formed from the place name – a so-called back formation), Pettistree ('Peohtrēd's tree'), Rickinghall, Inferior and Superior ('nook of the family or followers of Rīca' and a unique Suffolk way of saying Great

and Little Rickinghall), Southwold ('south forest'), Witnesham ('Wittīn's homestead'), Sutton Hoo ('southern farmstead on a ridge') and Wetheringsett-cum-Brockford ('the settlers of Weder's tribe by a ford').

Such place-names demonstrate how important the Anglo-Saxons were in building the foundations of modern Suffolk, its people, speech, humour, etc. From here, the further west or north one travels, the more this influence diminishes until at the extreme margins, where the Celtic population remained or sought refuge, it virtually disappears, and this is reflected in the place-names. Look at the place-names of Cornwall, for example, and you will see very quickly that the -hams, -leys and -ings disappear completely, and only one -ton has survived: Launceston.

Added to Suffolk's Anglo-Saxon heritage, is a richness of other cultures, evidence of which is once again testified by the place-names. Earlier settlers, the Celts (the Iceni) and pre-Celts, are remembered in various place-names and river names in the county, such as Iken. Curiously, though, the Romans, although they stayed in the country for close on 400 years, left not one enduring Latin place-name. However, their mark on the physical landscape is often recorded in Anglo-Saxon place-names. Old English burg, for example, frequently refers to Roman fortifications (Burgh and Burstall had Roman forts, as did Grundisburgh), while Old English stræt specifically denoted a paved and therefore Roman road, and place-names like Stradbroke, Stradishall, Stratford St Andrew and Stratford St Mary came into existence.

After settlement by the Anglo-Saxons, incursions and eventual settlement by successive waves of Norse invaders were to leave their mark on the stock of Suffolk place-names. For example, the Old Scandinavian word bý 'farmstead' appears in names like Barnby and Risby ('the farmstead of B(j)arni', 'the farmstead among the brushwood (Old Scandinavian hris), respectively). More interestingly, perhaps, the two cultures come together in names like Flixton, Thrandeston, and Uggeshall – each formed with an Old Scandinavian personal name (Flik, Thrándr, and Uggeca, respectively) combined with an Old English topographic suffix (tūn 'farmstead', 'settlement' or halh 'nook of land'). Such blends can sometimes be puzzling: the Old Scandinavian word for street, gata is confusingly similar to Old English geat 'gap', 'gate', 'pass', and sometimes only close scrutiny of the topography of the place in question can settle which word is the more likely component of its name.

Finally, the Normans, too, left their mark, with names like Boulge ('heathland'), Capel ('chapel') St Andrew, and Capel St Mary – just another ingredient in the rich recipe that is Suffolk place-names.

The ingredients for Suffolk, may be the same in a few other places, but the quantities would be different, hence the marked regional differences. Suffolk could be: –

5lb Angles
4lb Saxons
2lb Normans
1 pint Danes
2 tablespoons Jutes
2 tablespoons Fresians
3 teaspoons Viking
1 teaspoon Celt
2 Romans beaten and whisked (vigorously)
Pinch of Dutch

Put all ingredients together, stir thoroughly for a rich mixture, and you end up with the Suffolk people, its dialect, its humour, in fact, its whole make up. Alter the quantities or leave some out, and the mixture will turn out very differently; so will the make-up of the people, including the dialect, and the place-names.

Humpty Dumpty

A Duzzy Look at

Nursery Rhymes

Little Miss Muffet

A Duzzy Look at Nursery Rhymes

Little Jack Horner

CHAPTER 3

Wot's In a Name?

When you see names like, Cameron, Jardine, McDuff, Mackay, and Stuart, you immediately think of Scotland, and names like Penhaligon, Tredinnick, Tremain, Trevelyan, and Trewhella are clearly Cornish.

Likewise, although less obviously, Suffolk has its quota of surnames which originated in the county and are still strongly associated with it. In late Anglo-Saxon and Norman times, Suffolk was the most densely populated area of the country. Since then many Suffolkers have moved around or out of the county, taking their surnames with them or acquiring them on the way. Some became known by the name of the place from whence they came. By the same token, some 'furreners' moved to Suffolk bringing their surnames with them or becoming identified by their place of origin.

English surnames fall into several categories, of which the most common are personal names, occupational names, place-names and topographical names, relationship names, and nicknames or by-names. The acquisition of surnames (and by the term *surname* is meant a second name borne by all the members of the same family and passed down from generation to generation) was a gradual, post-Conquest phenomenon, the motivation for which can only be guessed at.

This glossary of Suffolk surnames is a list of just some of the names recorded prior to 1200. It does not include the many obvious surnames from Suffolk settlements such as Blakenham, Bardwell, Bungay, Debenham, Halesworth, Needham, Orford, or Woodbridge. All the names listed are still in existence in Suffolk today.

Albins	'son of the white one'
Allston	from the Middle English personal name *Alstan*
Ainger	from an Old French or Norman personal name
Branch	'branch', possibly denoting an offspring or descendent

Bullard	probably a nickname from a word meaning 'deceit' hence a cheat
Candler	'candle maker', a variant of Chandler
Cheek	nickname from a word meaning 'jaw-bone', possibly for someone with a protruding jaw
Copping	possibly denoting someone who lived on a hill top
Crisp	nickname for someone with curly hair
Faiers	nickname meaning 'fair', 'beautiful'; variant **Fayers**
Fulcher	from a personal name ('people' + 'army')
Griggs	'son of Gregory' or 'son of the dwarf'
Hunting	from a derivative of the Old English personal name *Hunta* 'hunter'
Hurren	nickname for someone with tousled hair
Keable	either a cudgelmaker or a nickname for someone stocky
Kerridge	from a Middle English personal name ('family' + 'ruler')
Munnings	probably 'son of Munda' ('protector')
Rump	'buttock', hence probably a derogatory nickname
Sorrell	from an Old French word meaning 'reddish brown', probably a descriptive nickname
Staff	nickname for a lean person
Stammers	either from the place-name Stanmore or from a personal name ('stone' + 'fame')
Stittle	probably a nickname for a belligerent or clumsy person
Strutt	possibly from an Old Norse byname or from a Middle English word meaning 'quarrel' and hence a nickname for an argumentative person
Thurkettle	from a derivative of an Old Norse personal name ('Thor' + 'kettle')
Turtill	shortened form of **Thurkettle**
Woolnough	from a personal name ('wolf' + 'boldness')
Worts	a vegetable seller
Whybrow	from a female personal name ('war' + 'fortress')

CHAPTER 4

Dicksh'nree

This is a glossary of Suffolk words. A few words may be used in some other dialects; a few may be archaic English words, but still commonly used in Suffolk. A few are ordinary English words with a different Suffolk meaning. Some just pure plain Suffolk. It is not, however, a list of Suffolk pronounciations of ordinary English words.

abroad   outside the local vicinity
Oi doont loike 'at 'air raype seed close boy, better off abroad.

absy   an abscess

addle   1. to save up (money)
At took me years t'addle up enough bor ferra week-end in Flixstowe.
2. to grow or thrive
'At gaard'n 'ont addle wi' all 'em 'air weeds agrow'n.

airy-wiggle   the earwig
(from Old English *earwicga*, a compound of *eare* 'ear' + *wicga*, probably related to *wiggle*, so named because it was thought to crawl into people's ears)

alp or blood alp   the bullfinch

arsel   1. to move backwards
2. (usually followed by *about*) to fidget whilst sitting down
Cood blaarst; 'ay aars'l about fairly. 'Ay must hev ants in th' pants.

arselins   backwards
Oi want yew a goo'n forruds, not aarsl'ns.

bab   crab or eel bait consisting of worms strung or tied together.

alp

babbing	crabbing or eeling using a *bab* tied to a weight on the end of a line (Walberswick still hosts the World Championships.) *He caught hell 'n' all th'uther day when he went a'babb'n.*
backus	a wash-house or scullery at the back of a farm house; a place for odd-jobs
backus boy	an odd-job boy *Oi started out on th' farm azza back'ss booy.*
baffled	to be knocked and twisted irregularly together *'At barley wuz hooly baaffl'd boy 'at owd storm laars noight.*
bang	a type of cheese made in Suffolk from milk skimmed several times; as a consequence it is very hard. Also known as **Suff'k thump**. It has poetically been described as 'Too large to swallow and too hard to bite'.
bargain	a quantity; a load *'At wuz a poor baarg'n o' wool from three score hoggets.*
barley bird	the nightingale *The baarlee bud, 'at hooly sing at noight. Bootaful sow'nd – th' lead singer in naytcher's kwoire.*
barley mung	barley meal mixed with water and milk to fatten up fowls or pigs *'Ont git enny aylm'nts feed'n em pigs 'at baarlee mung.*
bay duck	1. the shell duck 2. having bright colours like a bay horse
beastlings	the first milk drawn after a cow has calved *Cood blaarst, 'at beastl'ns pudd'ns better'an 'at mayde from orrd'nree milk, 'at 'at is.*
beavers	a four o'clock snack for farm workers still out in the fields (originally, it denoted horse feed) *Owd beavers kept me agoo'n ferra whoile longer.*
beazlings	the milk drawn from a cow after the *beastlings*, up to the fourth time
betty(-ass)	a female ass
betty boil	tea kettle
betty tit	the female tom tit or tittlemouse

barley bird

bibble   to eat like a duck searching for food in shallow water; to drink and eat at the same time

Bishop Barnabee   a ladybird; so called because, long ago, this particular bishop wore bright red and black attire. Usually shortened to **bishy**
Little owd bishy dun a lot o' good in th' gaard'n.

blob   blunt and rounded; said of something when it should be sharp or pointed
Poor owd booy. Hee's gotta blob nose, 'n' blob lips, 'n' his fingers are blob ended. No wunda he 'ent gotta little owd mawther.

blowbroth   a meddling old busy body

blote-herring   a bloater
   (*bloaterr'n*)

bobble   fuss or worry
Yew mayke a bobble 'bowt north'n, yew dew.

bonnka   a fine, strapping, well-built young person, especially a girl
'At mawther's a rare bonnka.

Workers enjoying beavers (Suffolk Record Office – ref. K681.122.35)

botty big headed
Cood blaarst, shee's a botty little owd madam.

bor a friendly form of address between men or boys
How dew yew fare, bor? Dew yew keep a'throsh'n, bor? 'Taint be ser loikley, bor.

boud a biscuit weevil
 (bowd) *Yew hatter tap 'em owd bowds out afore yew eat 'em bisc'ts.*

brattlings tree loppings and toppings used in hurdles or for hedging or firing

brawtch a bent hazel stick used as a staple to secure a *rizzer* (rod) *or to hold in straw or reed on a thatched roof*

brew the edge of a ditch away from a hedge

brummager a seafarer who pilots boats without a licence

bumby a hole dug outside the back door for depositing kitchen waste before it is put on the compost
Cood blaast, 'at bumby hooly stinks; needs clear'n owt.

buttle the bittern

caddow the jackdaw

capper 1. the skin that forms on boiled milk, custard, rice pudding, etc. when it is cooled
2. the surface of soil when it has suddenly dried after rain

caddow

carr a wetland copse, normally of alders

cavings the chaff collected from a threshing floor
 (cayv'ns)

chates scraps; leftover food
Dew yew eat 'em 'air chates – nuth'n till t'morrer.

clent cleaned
Oi clent up th' back'ss, whilst yew wuz a'gone.

clung 1. dried up fruit and vegetables that have gone rubbery
2. dry, tough bread made from wheat that has sprouted

coach a baby's pram or carrycot

cock's egg	a small misshapen egg (from Middle English *cokeney*)
comb (*coom*)	a quantity of variable weight of wheat, beans, peas, etc., usually in a sack
crew	crowed *'At 'air cockr'll; 'at hooly crew laars noight.*
daddle	to walk like a young child trying to copy its father
dag	low fog or mist; dew *Yew cood see yer footprints in th' dag 'smorn'n.*
dannocks	protective gloves worn by hedgers and haywards: the left hand was a glove of thick leather, designed for holding the vegetation, and the right hand a leather mitten for handling a bill hook or other cutting tool
dauzy	confused. Also, **duzzy.** *'At 'air mod'n moozic; 'at mayke a duzzy din, 'at 'at doo!*
deeve	to dive; to dip *Yew marn't deeve yer hands inter 'at boil'n waarter.*
develing (**deevl'n**)	the swift (so called because of the way it dives)
dicky(-ass)	a male ass
dicky dilver	the periwinkle
diddle	a young duck; a suckling pig; any youngster. Also **diddlings**.
diddling	faring *'Woop bor! How a' yew a' diddl'n?'*
dill	a pap of a female pig
dobble	a clod of mud or earth; a lump of snow formed on the heels of shoes or boots
doddy	small in stature; often a nickname for a small person. Also **dood**, **doody**. *'At coot'll bee too large fer owd Doddy.*
dodman	see **hodman**
doke	a shallow hole made in the ground, such as a footprint
door stall	a doorpost
dop	to curtsey
dorkey	elevenses; a mid-morning snack

doxy
a mistress
'Th' owd sqoire's gotta doxy a two.'

drawling
to dawdle, idle about. Also **drawlatch**.
Hee'll git th' sack afore long, keep on a' drawlin' loike he do.

drindle
a small water channel taking water off a road into a ditch

driv
drove
Oi driv t' Ipsidge 'n' back yessdee.

dullor
a noise
'At mod'n moozic, 'at mayke a hellava dullor.

dungy
not very good:
'At wuz a dungy thing t'do, bor, roight naarsty.

dussent
should not, but somewhat stronger, close on dare not
Yew dussent goo a'scrump'n in th' orch'd.

dwile
a floorcloth made from **dwiling**, a rough flannel

A farm worker having his dorkey

33

A thatcher 'roiv'n th' brawtches with a flasher'.
(Suffolk Record Office, ref. K681.1.348.3)

dwile flunking floorcloth throwing
A serious, competitive game of East Anglia, it is played between two teams, with the sole purpose of drinking vast quantities of ale and ending up very merry. In days gone by, the game was usually played to celebrate the end of harvest; nowadays, it is played for fund-raising and fun.

dwinge to shrivel up
Fruit like apples will *dwinge* if kept too long

ebble the aspen tree

ecclestree a crossbar or rod supporting a vehicle or cart

ewe owed
He ewe me a foiver fer two year a' more afore he pay'd me back.

fairly a lot; a great deal
'At rained fairly s'morn'n.

fay out to clean out, especially a ditch, pond, dyke, **bumby**, or the like
Oi'll hatter fay out 'at owd ditch 'at hooly corze a stench.

flack(y) to hang loose

flacket a girl, usually quite tall and slender, who flounces about in loose hanging clothes

flash to trim a hedge
Yew'll hatter wear sum dann'ks t' flash 'at 'air hedge.

flasher any of the tools used to **flash**, such as a reaping hook or sickle
Dew yew keep yer flashers sharp, bor.

fogger a pedlar, tinker, or street seller
The term is often used as a nickname, sometimes in the form *Foggy*.
Hatter tell owd Fogger Whymonger moy flashers need a' sharpn'n.

fore horse see **thill horse**

frawn very cold
Cood-a-hell Oi wuz frawn roight throo; 'ose easterlies hooly blew.

froise a pancake
(froiz) *Moy owd muther, she mayke a best froizs row'nd heeya fer moiles, bor.*

The fogger was a welcome visitor to the villages in the late 19th century

furrener	anyone born outside the local area, especially someone from outside Suffolk
galloped-beer	a small quantity of beer brewed for immediate use, by ***galloping*** (boiling) small quantities of hops and malt together in a kettle
gay gotch	a large round jug with a handle
gentle	a bluebottle larva (maggot) used for fishing bait *Moy boy; he stick 'em gentles under his tunge t' mayke 'em wiggle afore he puts 'em on th hook; dutty dav'l.*
gig	a silly, lighthearted man The term is often used as a nickname.
good tidily	quite a few; several
good tidily sum	more than several
grip, gripple	see ***groop***

groop   a large **drindle** for allowing water to run off lanes into ditches. Also **grup**.
A narrow **groop** is called a **grip**; narrower than that is a **gripple**, though there is no exact science to establish the difference between them.

gussock   a strong and sudden force of wind; a gust
'At 'air guss'k fare t' knock me off moy boike.

hackle   to restrain farm animals to stop them from absconding, usually by strapping together the front or back pair of legs

haggy   newly ploughed soil, being a rough and uneven surface but still with a shiny moist surface

harnser   the heron. Also **harnsey**.
My father spoke of a place in Snape, down by the river, called The Harnser, because of the number of herons found there.

hawkey   a feast at the end of harvest

hay   a hedge

hayjack   the reed warbler

haysel(e)   the season for making hay

haywarding   the act of laying or **flashing** a hedge by pruning, bending, and interlocking the branches to form a growing, stockproof barrier

hew   hoed
Oi hew th' gaard'n yessdee 'n' moi baack 'at hooly give me jip.

hisself   himself

hodman   a snail. Also **dodman**, **hodmadod**.

hogget   a young sheep, a yearling, after first shearing
(hogg't)

hold you hard   a plea for caution, with the sense 'wait a minute', 'let's think'
Howd yew haard, bor, else 'att'll be a duzzy do.

hooly   fairly; very. Also **hully**.
'At's hooly cowd.
'At's a hooly good point a' ale.
'At 'air wind fare t' hooly blow.

Workers at haysel time (Suffolk Record Office, ref. K681.1.5.20)

holl	a dry ditch
hopple	to hobble; compare **hackle**
hornpie	the peewit
	In Suffolk, as elsewhere, this bird is also known as a lapwing and green plover – good cause for an identity crisis, I reckon.
huh	skew; slant
	'At 'air pitcher en't hang'n roight. 'At's sloightly on th' huh.
hully	see **hooly**
hutkin	a cot or sheath to cover a sore finger
imitate	to make an unsuccessful attempt
	He immertayte at work'n.
	She immertayte at play'n th' pee'anner.
jacob	a toad, especially a large one. Also **jakey**
jasper	a wasp
jammock	to beat to a pulp
(jamm'k)	

*This picture of a fishing smack leaving
Lowestoft harbour c.1900 is 'sloightly on th' huh'.
(Suffolk Record Office, ref. K681.1.310.87)*

jink	to sprain a joint, muscle, etc. *Oi hooly jinked moi ankle a' tripp'n oover 'at stoon.*
jip	to gut a herring
jipper	a gutted herring
jumble	a drink composed of equal quantities of ale and stout *A point a' jumble plees, landlord.*
kedgy	active; alive; alert. Also **kedge**. *'How dew yew fare?' 'Kedgy 'n' well, bor.'*
kiddier	a travelling trader who buys and sells farm produce and fowls. Also **kidger**.

King Harry — the goldfinch

knap-kneed — knock-kneed

lagarag — an idler

lapbag — a large pouch used by gleaners for collecting corn off a field after harvesting

lark horse — see *thrill horse*

larn — to teach
'At'll laarn yer.
This is a common dialect phrase in Suffolk and elsewhere, often ridiculed by the 'educated', who think it means 'That will learn you.' In fact it comes from an Old English word sharing a common origin with modern German *lehren* 'to teach'.

lijah
(*loijer*) — a leg strap worn below the knee by farm labourers

ligger — a line with a float and bait, so designed to be left to lie in the water for some time in order to catch pike

Long Melford
(*Long Mellf't*) — a long stocking-shaped purse made of soft leather. It is depicted on the village sign.

lorker — a seagull

lugsome — heavy; cumbersome
Cood blaarst. 'At barr'll o' ale fare t' be hooly lugs'm.

maggoty — pernickety, fastidious
She be too maggoty t'eat stoo 'n' dumpl'ns.

A harvester wearing his lijahs (Suffolk Record Office, ref. SPS 7302)

mardle	1. a nearby pond, convenient for feeding cattle
	2. to gossip: *He hooly mardle bowt all on uss.*
marn't	must not
	Yew marn't goo owtsoide inniss wether, bor.
marster	excellent; the very best
	She did a marster job on 'at 'air embroydree.
	Cood blaarst, Oi grew sum marster tayters 'is sees'n.
maund	a large basket used in fishing or one carried on the chest for broadcasting seed
mavis	the song thrush. Also **mavish**.
mawther	an adolescent girl, before womanhood; a girlfriend
	Oi'll hatter tell moy lill owd mawther she'll hatter cumma long wi' mee.
mawthering	excessive cuddling or fussing over a male by any female
	'At mayke yer cuss t' see her a'mawther'n him th'way she do.
mazy	giddy and dizzy
meetiner	a person who goes to religious meetings; a Nonconformist

Southwold fishermen with their 'maunds' (Suffolk Record Office, ref. SPS.12973 [S80])

mentle   a woman's coarse woollen apron

mew   mowed
He mew th'law'n yessdee.

mucher (is not a)   sub-standard, no good, bad
'Woont boy 'at owd second-hand car.' 'Cood blaarst, 'at ent a mutcher.'

muddled   tired out
Arter 'at walk along 'at 'air beach, Oi'm muddled fairly.

nabbity   a short full-grown woman

nab-nanny   the head louse

nannocking   to idle about; play the fool
Oi caarnt be a' work'n wi' he; th'way hees a'nannerk'n so.

native   birthplace
Ipsidge 's moy nayt'ff.

nettus   cowhouse, byre

nevvied-up   exhausted, tired out; **muddled**

nigh-nor-by   near
'At's too layte. Shee ont cum noy-nor-boy now

Noah's Ark   a clear cloud formation forecasting rain later

noonings   a farm labourer's midday meal. Also **nunins**.

nuddle   to walk alone with the head held low
Suffen up wi' he, nuddl'n along loike he do

nuttery stub   a clump of hazel bushes

ont   won't
He own't do 'at inner munth a Sundees.

ought   nought, nil, zero
Ipsidge Town beat Norrudge three ort. Th' year, two thows'nd, woz th' year a three orts.

oven bird   the long tailed tit, so called because of its oven-shaped nest

paigle   the cowslip
She mayke maarster payg'l woine; 'at tayste hooly good, 'at do.

pamment   a square paving tile or brick

pample   to walk heavily, leaving footprints; to trample
We were pampl'n acrorst th' dag.

parney	to rain heavily *'At parney fairly.*
pawt	one of a pair of flat boards attached to the feet for walking across mudflats or very wet soil
ped	a large wicker basket with a lid, used by a **pedder** to carry merchandize to sell
peterman	a fisherman
pighle	a small enclosed area of land large enough to keep a pig for a year Many houses and cottages in Suffolk are named *Pighle*. I wonder if their occupants know what it means.
pin horse	see ***thill horse***
pingle	to move food about on the plate for want of an appetite *Yew ont git biggen strong keep a' pingl'n yor food so.*
pleating	to strengthen the hedge tops during the process of haywarding
podge	fat bellied, sometimes **pod**
polliwiggle	a tadpole
pork cheese	brawn, made from pig's face, trotters, etc.
potchet	1. pottery made out of broken earthenware 2. an earthenware egg to put under a hen to induce her to lay *Hoop 'at potch't works, else 'at hen ont be a mutcher.*
proper	excellent, exact, as it's supposed to be *'At's a proper pub.*
puggle	to wash clothes inadequately.
puggy	badly washed; still dirty *Doont yew give 'em clothes a pug wash; ont want'em puggy afore'n' after*
pulk	a muddy waterhole
pundletree (*pummel tree*)	a wooden cross bar to attach horses to a plough or harrow
pungled	(of fruit that has been kept too long) tough and shrivelled but not gone rotten
push	a pimple, blister, or boil

SLOIGHTLY ON TH' HUH!

quackle	to choke *He hooly quackl'd arter he kwoff'd his ale.*
quarrel	usually a square piece of glass
queach	set-aside land; land which is too bushy and rough to till
quoddle	to boil gently, especially eggs before pickling
rabs	large clumsy feet
rafty	1. cold, dank, raw weather *Cood blaarst bor, 'at's hooly raarfty 's' morn'n.* 2. stale, stagnant
ranny	the shrew; someone with a long snout
ranter	a beer can; originally, a copper or tin vessel for carrying beer from the cellar to the bar
rattick	a very loud noise *'Ay mayke a helluva ratt'ck; mayke moy ears sake.*
ringle	1. to put a ring through a bull's or pig's snout 2. the ring itself *Ringle thy hog, or look for a dog.* (Tusser)
risp	the stalk or stem of a climbing plant such as the runner bean, pea, etc.
rive (roive)	to split wood, especially **brawtches**
riving beetle	a large wooden hammer used to split logs by driving wooden wedges into them
rizzer	a narrow strip of wood used to lay down thatch held in by **brawtches**
roke	a fog or mist across sea, wetlands, or marsh
rokey	misty, foggy *Cood blaarst, bor, 'at's hooly rokey 's' morn'n*
rommock	to romp vigorously *'Ose young lambs, 'ay romm'ck fairly.*
rove (roove)	a partially formed scab on a bloody wound or sore
rub	a whetstone for sharpening the cutting edge of a tool
runned	ran *Oi runned fer th' buss 'n' missed th' bugger.*

The harvest team – the men all holding their 'rubs' to sharpen the scythes

ruttle to breathe heavily and noisily
Poor owd booy, herd'm ruttl'n moile off.

sale either of the two curved wooden or metal pieces forming part of a horse's collar

sally the hare
(via Norman French from Latin *salire* 'to leap')

sappy dim, silly, foolish
'Ee's a sappy lumm'x

sarnick to loiter or dawdle
How he sarnick along, loike a bluddy snayle.

sauzles a semi-liquid food comprising a mixture of vegetables and herbs. Also **sawzles**.

sawny silly, foolish; **sappy**, **duzzy**
What a sawny owd hayp'th.

SLOIGHTLY ON TH' HUH!

scranch	to make a grinding noise. Also **scrawnch**. *He hooly scrornch when he eat.* *He ent ever driv' a tractor afore; he scrornch'd 'em gears fairly.*
shew	showed *Owd booy on th' farm shew me wot t'do.* *Th'owd vicar shew me th' way.*
shrick	shrieked. Also **shruck**. *'At baybee, 'at hooly shrick afore 'ats feed'n toime.*
shunt	to get rid of *How he sarnick'd along. Oi suun got shunt a' hee.*
skep	a wooden or wicker basket e.g. a coal skep
slummock	an untidy person
slummock along	to walk in an ungainly or clumsy fashion
smeaky	going off, slightly tainted, especially of meat, bacon, or ham *'At streaky's a bit smeaky.*
snack	a traditional, thumb-operated doorlatch. Also **snick**.
soling	1. a thrashing *Oi gotta hooly good sole'n fer scrump'n 'em 'air apples.* 2. a vigorous tugging of someone's ear
sosh (on the)	crooked, slanting; compare **huh**
spadger	the sparrow
spadgering	the act of catching sparrows using a net placed over a hedge or stack, an activity usually carried out at dusk
spink	the chaffinch
spong	1. a narrow strip of land 2. a bridleway
squit	complete and utter nonsense *'At looc'l cownsler, he do talk a lood a squit.*
stroop	the windpipe or gullet
suffen	something *Oi tell yew suff'n else, 'n' 'at's a fact.*
sussucka	a clout, a blow *Oi give he a helleva susserker a'hoind th' lugs.*

46

thill hoss   pin hoss   lark hoss   fore hoss

thill horse	the horse (*hoss*) in a team that goes 'twixt the shafts. Also **thiller**. The **fore horse** is followed by the **lark horse**, then the **pin horse**, and finally the **thill horse**.
tizzick	a dry cough
together	a very common form of address to people as a group or individually *Come along t'gather.* *We'll hatter goo in one atter toime t'gather.* *Cheerio t'gather.*
tricolate	to decorate, adorn *At spring toime, th' blossom hooly trickerlate th' hedgerows.*
twiddle	a small pimple
twizzling stick	a stick used to flatten beer/ale that is too gassy or lively by giving it a twizzle or stir

SLOIGHTLY ON TH' HUH!

wapsy	a wasp
water whelp	a heavy dumpling
wet bird	the green woodpecker
wisp	a handful of straw folded over and knotted to temporarily plug a hole in a sack
without	unless
	Oi marnt goo t'mark't withowt yew come along 'n' all.
woodsprite	the spotted woodpecker
yelm	straw divided into convenient bundles for use by a thatcher
yip	to chirp and sing like a newly hatched bird

Ixworth Thorpe church being thatched. Note the yelms at the bottom of the picture.

CHAPTER 5

Peculiarly Suffolk

THE SUFFOLK PUNCH

The Suffolk Punch is probably the oldest pure heavy horse breed in the British Isles; its history can be traced back to 1506, though its development undoubtedly dates back much further. All animals alive today can be traced in the male line to a stallion called Crisp's Horse of Ufford, foaled in 1768. The Suffolk Punch is a very beautiful animal, and is invariably chestnut colour, though it can be any one of seven shades, the most common being bright chestnut, with a thin white blaze down the face. The shape of the breed – a big body, with a girth of over 8 feet, and short legs – gives it its strength and its name, punch being an old Suffolk term

Farriers at Stratford St Mary (Suffolk Record Office, ref. SPS 9333)

for short and stocky. The legs are clean with no feathers. Their temperament is very good, and they have a long working life, ideal for hard work. Old Suffolkers say that Suffolk Punches have 'the face of an angel, a belly like a barrel, and an arse like a Suffolk farmer's daughter's'. Well I know a fair few Suffolk farmers' daughters, and I can tell you ... no ... p'raps I oughtn't.

In 1794 a Northumberland farmer, Geo. Culley described Suffolk Punches thus:-

'It is probable their merit consists more in constitutional hardiness than true shape, being in general a very plain made horse; their colour large, ears wide, muzzle coarse, fore-end low, back long but very straight, sides flat, shoulders too far forward, hind quarters middling, but rather high above the hips, legs round and short in the pasterns, deep bellied, full in the flank.'

Although it is obvious that Geo. Culley did not like the look of a Suffolk Punch, he had to concede, however that 'these horses do perform a surprising day's work; it is well known that the Suffolk farmers plough more land in a day, than any other people in the island and these are the kind of horses everywhere used in the district'.

THE CRINKLE-CRANKLE WALL

There are roughly 70 crinkle-crankle or crinkley-crankley walls listed throughout England. There are a handful in north Essex and south Norfolk, and one or two elsewhere; the rest are in Suffolk.

The Dutch designed and started building them when they were invited over to help to reclaim and drain low-lying land. Crinkle-crankle walls are usually one brick thick and rise to just over 6 feet in height; their distinguishing feature is the way they wind in and out. The concept is simple, but ingenius; the undulations mean that such walls are self-supporting and need no plinths or pillars. An added bonus is that on the sunny side of the wall exotic plants and fruits can be grown in the sheltered curves.

SUFFOLK HAMS AND BACONS

Black treacle bacon and gammons, known colloquially as *black'ns*, are truly peculiarly Suffolk.

Ever since black or brown sugar started coming into England, black'ns have been produced in Suffolk, and, thankfully, production continues to this day, albeit in only one or two places. The taste is unique.

When I visited F.E. Neave & Son, in Debenham, to get the 'low down', I was given a conducted tour, shown the production method, and given some of the recipe.

'Owd' Mr Neave delivering the 'black'ns'

The butcher's shop is still in Debenham today

The prepared bacon and boned joints are given a brine cure. They are then steeped in brine, with black treacle, brown sugar, and – wait for it – stout, plus a handful of this and a handful of that. I instinctively knew not to ask what these handfuls were; these were the secret ingredients that produced the company's particular taste and were not to be made public, rightly so. The bellies and the bacons are left in this glorious mixture for one month, and the gammons for five to six weeks. They are then taken out, hung up to dry, and then smoked – either with oak, for a stronger taste, or beech, for a more subtle taste.

This particular establishment has become famous, not only in Suffolk, but further afield, and has been the subject of radio and TV programmes, a feature in *The Times* and endless other publications. So popular are the Suffolk hams and bacons from F.E. Neave & Son, that a very successful mail order business has built up, especially with vacuum packing. Some very famous, well established, high class restaurants and top-notch customers are on the mailing list.

Suffolk hams and bacons are now being enjoyed all over Great Britain and abroad. Hooly good!

SUFFOLK WHITE BRICKS

This type of brick is not made anywhere else. It was used to build the Law Courts, Covent Garden Opera House, the Royal Albert Hall, and many more prestigious buildings in London and throughout England. Indeed, legend has it that two very famous white buildings in the United States of America were built with Suffolk whites from Woolpit. Who am I to disagree?

In the river valleys throughout Suffolk, mixed in with the silts that were washed down to form clay was a high proportion of chalk, resulting in a brick that on being fired turned a creamy white. This unique clay mix occurs only in Suffolk. Throughout the ages, the method of production hardly changed, until the mid-1700s, when the dictates of fashion decreed that a white brick for the front elevations of buildings was most prestigious. Thereafter, the clay was washed of

Suffolk White Brick kilnworkers (Suffolk Record Office, ref. SPS 2302)

all impurities, and a slurry of either a chalk or lime was added to produce a very white brick.

The brick is of a very high quality and is particularly good for elaborate decoration. The dimensions, however, do not conform to the standard brick measurements. In fact, each company, of which there were once many, would produce to its own specifications. Sadly, the majority of these companies have disappeared, techniques have altered, and the source of clay has changed. But the Suffolk white is still being produced, although purists would argue that only bricks made using the methods and raw materials of the mid-1700s could claim to be the genuine article.

SUFFOLK PINK

Throughout Suffolk, umpteen cottages are painted in what is called Suffolk pink. There are a great number of theories written about this colour, and many are misleading; it's time now to put the record straight.

In fact, the colour is a dark red rather than pink, and pig's blood is among the ingredients. However, the blood has little to do with the colour; so why was it

SLOIGHTLY ON TH' HUH!

added? And what gives Suffolk 'pink' its hue? The answer is simple: to add colour to the limewash, red ochre is added; and, in order to give the wash stability and stop it flaking once applied, a binding material is added, in this case, pigs' blood. The blood, once spilled, turns a browny colour, and so, when added to the mix, has a tendency to darken the colour if anything. The popular misconception that the blood determines the colour, however, still persists.

SUFFOLK STEEL QUOITS

The game of quoits is said to have originated in India, with the Sikhs, who used sharp throwing rings as weapons.

Quoits have come a long way since then, and in medieval times in England the game was played in one form or another at festivals, in hostelries, and on village greens.

Suffolk was no exception. Gradually Suffolk formed its own set of rules, had its own leagues, and, by the late 1800s and early 1900s, nearly every village had its steel quoit team. Many trophies were competed for, the most famous being the Lord Rendlesham Challenge Cup, which is made of solid silver. It is still competed

The Brockford Quoits Team of 1911 (Suffolk Record Office, ref. K681/1/493/7)

Players proudly displaying the Lord Rendlesham Challenge Cup (courtesy of the Holbrook Swan)

SLOIGHTLY ON TH' HUH!

for today. Sadly the pastime has declined, but there are two leagues still in existence, namely, Hadleigh and District and Stoke by Nayland and District.

The game is played on a clay pitch. A 'light', normally, a thin strip of white paper, is placed in the clay to show the location of the pin below.

Some of the rules for Suffolk steel quoits:

1. The pitch shall be 18 yards clear. The player shall deliver his quoits with both feet behind the toe board, and must not step over the toe board. Players must leave the pitching zone to the rear. If a quoit shall alight more than 18 inches from the pin or shall be inclined backwards, it shall be called a *no quoit* and withdrawn.

2. The top of the pin shall measure $\frac{5}{8}$ inch to $\frac{3}{4}$ inch, and shall have a $\frac{1}{8}$ inch hole in the top.

3. Quoits shall not exceed $7\frac{1}{4}$ lbs per pair, $7\frac{1}{4}$ inches in diameter.

4. Any quoit covering any part of the top of the pin to be called a *cover*, and to count before a *side-toucher*.

5. All ringers to be withdrawn and count 2 points. No quoit to count a ringer if a quoit under it is a cover.

6. In the case of ringers from each team, ringers count, nothing else.

7. Anything not covered by these rules will be dealt with by the committee, whose decision is final.

There are similar games in Yorkshire and Wales, but both have different size quoits, shorter pitches, and different rules. The Suffolk rules are unique and altogether removed from the others, making Suffolk steel quoits unquestionably peculiarly Suffolk.

CHAPTER 6

The Suffolk Kitchen

SUFFOLK RUSKS

       8 oz/250 g plain flour
       3 level teasp./15 ml baking powder
       small pinch of salt
       3 oz/75 g butter
       1 oz/25 g lard
       1 egg, beaten
       milk to mix, approx. 2 tablesp. (60 ml)

1. A hot quick oven is required, so pre-set to 230°C, 450°F or Gas Mark 8.
2. Mix the flour, baking powder, and salt, and then sift into a bowl.
3. Slice the butter and rub into the mixture until it feels like fine bread crumbs; this *must* take at least 10 minutes – no short cuts!
4. Add the beaten egg and enough milk to make a soft smooth dough.
5. Roll out the dough on a floured surface to 1 inch (2.5 cm) thick.
6. Cut out 2½ inch (6 cm) rounds and place them on a greased baking tray.
7. Cook for 10 minutes, and then remove from oven.
8. Turn the oven down to 190°C, 375°F or Gas Mark 5.
9. Split the rounds in half by pulling them apart with two forks, and replace them, cooked side down, in the oven for another 10 minutes.
10. When golden brown and crisp, remove from the oven and place on cooling rack.

When to eat: at *fourses*, with jam and butter, or with cheese.

The herrings catch at Lowestoft in 1901 (Suffolk Record Office, ref. SPS 14407 [S65])

SUFFOLK BOILED HERRING

12 herrings, all *clent* up (gutted and cleaned)

3 pints/1½ litres seawater

1. Boil the seawater
2. Place the herrings in the boiling water and boil for 10 minutes.
3. Remove and drain.

When to eat: as a main meal, with potatoes and peas (or greens).

SUFFOLK BREAD AND ONION PUDDING

8 oz/225 g bread (sliced)

2 oz/50 g finely chopped onion

salt and pepper

1 teasp./5 ml sage

¾ pt/400 ml milk

2 eggs, beaten

1. Put the slices of bread on a baking tray; bake in a slow oven (250°F, 120°C), until they are crisp and dry.
2. Remove from the oven and crush with a rolling pin; then push through a sieve.
3. Place the toasted crumbs (raspings) in a bowl and add the onions and other ingredients. Mix thoroughly.
4. Place in a greased baking tin, and bake in a hot quick oven (400°F, 200°C, Gas Mark 6) for 30 minutes.

When to eat: slice the pudding and eat, covered with gravy, with a main meal in place of dumplings.

OXTAIL BRAWN (SUFFOLK'S ANSWER TO PORK CHEESE)

1 oxtail, jointed
1 oz/25 g butter
1 made-up herb and spice bag with own choices
(*usually parsley, thyme, sage, and cloves*)
1 peeled onion, whole
salt and pepper to season
2 tablesp./60 ml vinegar
1 coddled egg, shelled and sliced
seasoned flour

(*To coddle an egg; place it in a pan of cold water and bring the water to the boil. At that point, put the lid on the saucepan and remove it from heat; allow to stand for 15 minutes. The egg slowly cooks (coddles) in the water.*)

1. Sprinkle the oxtail joints with the seasoned flour.
2. Melt the butter in a deep frying pan and fry the oxtail until just brown on both sides.
3. Add the vinegar, onion, seasoning, and sufficient cold water to cover. Now add the herb/spice bag.
4. Bring to the boil and simmer gently for 4 to 4½ hrs.
5. Take off the heat, cool, and remove the meat; chop it thoroughly and put to one side.

6. Keep the stock with the bones, but remove the onion and herb bag.

7. Smear a pudding basin with butter and place the slices of egg on the bottom. (Do not double up.)

8. Add the chopped meat.

9. Bring the stock with the bones back to the boil, and simmer until it is reduced to about ½ pint.

10. Allow the liquid to cool and strain into the basin. Cover with a plate.

11. Put in the larder or down in the cellar until cold and set.

When to eat: at teatime or for a summer lunch. Slice the brawn and eat with cooked vegetables.

SUFFOLK HARD DUMPLING

This popular dish was used as *befores*, or served with the main meal, or for *afters*, as a sweet pudding.

> 8 oz/225 g plain flour
> pinch of salt
> approx. ½ pint/250 ml of cold water
> 1 oz/25 g currants (to serve as a pudding)

1. Mix the flour, water, and salt (and currants, if used) together and kneed into a firm dough.

2. On a floured board, roll into six equal-sized balls.

3. Place into a pan of boiling water.

4. Replace the lid and continue to boil on a high heat for 20 minutes.

5. Remove and drain.

When to eat: as a starter, pulled apart with two forks and covered in gravy; as a dumpling with a main meal; or as a sweet, with melted butter on the top and a generous sprinkling of brown sugar – once again, pulled apart with two forks. (We did have knives in Suffolk, but we didn't use them with dumplings or rusks.)

SUFFOLK BEAVERS CURRANT BREAD (CAKE)

$^3/_4$ lb/340 g strong flour

pinch of salt

$^1/_4$ oz/6 g fresh yeast (or dried, if not available)

1 teasp./5 ml mixed spice

1 teasp./5 ml sugar

$^3/_8$ pint/250 ml warm water

3 oz/75 g lard

3 oz/75 g currants

1. Mix the strong flour, salt, and mixed spices together, and sift into a bowl.
2. Slice the lard and rub into the mixture.
3. Make a separate mixture with the yeast, sugar, and a tablespoon of the water. Mix to a creamy texture.
4. Make a hollow in the flour mixture and add the yeast mixture with the remaining water.
5. Mix thoroughly to a smooth dough, and add the currants.
6. Put on a floured surface and kneed thoroughly.
7. Cover and leave in a warm place until doubled in size.
8. Knead lightly, and then place the dough in a greased 1 lb loaf tin, and leave to prove in a warm place until the dough has risen 1 inch/2.5 cm above the tin.
9. Cook in a pre-set hot quick oven (200°C, 400°F or Gas Mark 6) for 45 mins.

When to eat: originally eaten with or without butter at 4 o'clock (*fourses* or *beavers*) or during a break from working in the field.

CHAPTER 7

Folk Scene

Suffolk has a rich folk tradition which can still seen today in pubs and clubs throughout the county. There are regular organized as well as impromptu folk sessions, some unaccompanied and some featuring traditional musical instruments. History is kept alive through song, instrumental music, dance, and the spoken word.

There are numerous folk dancing clubs, a good many groups for morris dancers and also for molly dancers (similar to morris dancers but without the hankies, sticks and bells), and various other types of traditional dance. In addition, the county has its very own brand of dancing, known as Suffolk step dancing, as depicted by Percy Denny and one-eyed Syd Cook at the Eel's Foot pub at Eastbridge in 1940. Suffolk step dancers take their boards around with them, and, when the occasion arises, they place them on the floor and dance, especially at places like the Ship public house at Blaxhall, near Woodbridge, the Low House, Laxfield, the Bell at Middleton, the White Horse, Edwardstone and the Eel's Foot at Eastbridge.

Suffolk is well known for many folk songs, but there are two in particular which have become anthems almost throughout the folk scene in the county.

The Yellow Hankerchief
(or Flash Company)

> Once I loved a young girl as I loved my life,
> And thro' keeping flash company, has ruined my life,
> Has ruined my life, like a great many more.
> If it hadn't been for flash company, I'd never a been so poor.

Philip Lumpkin, with an old cribbage marker as a gavel, starts off the evening's entertainment at the Eel's Foot pub, Eastbridge, in December 1940 (courtesy of the Eastbridge Eel's Foot)

So take a yellow hankerchief in rememberance of me,
And tie it round my neck my love in flash company.
Flash company, my boys, like a great many more,
If it hadn't been for flash company, I'd never a been so poor.

For it's once I'd had a colour, as red as the rose,
But now I'm as pale as the lily that grows,
Like a flower in the garden, when all my colour's gone
Can't you see what I'm coming to, thro' loving that one.

(Chorus)

For it's fiddling and dancing has been my delight,
And along with those flash girls I spent every night.
Now my money's all gone, and my love lingers on,
Can't you see what I'm coming to, thro' loving that one.

(Chorus)

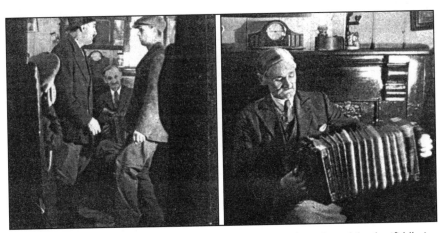

Percy Denny and one-eyed Syd Cook dancing their famous hornpipe whilst the 'fiddler',
Mr Button (centre and right), livens things up with his accordian (courtesy of the
Eastbridge Eel's Foot)

SLOIGHTLY ON TH' HUH!

The association with the sea has certainly made this next song very popular in Suffolk, and whenever it is sung the audience joins in. I remember my grandfather's version below:

The Faithful Sailor Boy

It was a dark and stormy night, the snow lay on the ground.
A sailor boy stood on the quay, his ship was outward bound.
His sweetheart standing by his side, shed many a silent tear,
And as he pressed her to his breast, he whispered in her ear.

Farewell, farewell, my own true love; this parting gives me pain.
I'll be your own true guiding star when I return again.
My thoughts shall be of you, of you, when storms are raging high.
Farewell my love, remember me, your faithful sailor boy.

Then with the gale the ship set sail, he kissed his love goodbye.
She watched the craft till out of sight, till tears bedimmed her eye.
She prayed to Him in heaven above, to guide him on his way.
Those loving parting words that night re-echoed o'er the bay.

(Chorus)

It's sad to say the ship returned without her sailor boy.
He died whilst on the voyage home: the flags flew half-mast high.
His comrades when they came on shore, told her that he was dead,
And a letter he had sent to her, those last lines sadly read.

Farewell, farewell, my own true love, on earth we'll meet no more.
I soon shall be from storm and sea on that eternal shore.
I hope to meet you in that land, that land beyond the sky,
Where you will ne'er be parted from your faithful sailor boy.

Poetry and verse are another popular form of folk culture in Suffolk, and it is very common in clubs and sessions to hear *mardles* and monologues, usually depicting some aspect of Suffolk life and history. This *mardle* and monologue, written and performed by myself, is a stand for the Suffolk dialect, and is included on my CD. It attempts to explain this common Suffolk saying: '**the best part a fair few**'.

The Mardle

On looking at a concise dictionary, what do you find?
> *few* – not many; less than several.
> *several* – more than two, but not many.

I prefer the more accurate *Inconcise Suffolk Dictionary*:
> *few* – not many; but a fair few is quite a number; that's more than a few, but not as much as *part a fair few*. A *part a fair few* is more than *a fair few*, although its only a part of, and its less than, *the best part a fair few*. The best part a fair few is more than *part a fair few*, and is a term for a large number; quite a few. An exact number can't be put to a *few, fair few, part a fair few,* or *best part a fair few,* as it depends on the items being discussed or referred to.

For example, take the number 14:

> 14 *matches* in a box would be a *few*.
> 14 *cigarettes* in a session at The Low House, Laxfield would be a *fair few*.
> 14 miles cycled from Debenham to Laxfield would be *part of a fair few*.
> 14 pints sunk in one session at the Edwardstone White Hoss, would be the *best part of a fair few*.

Now we look up the word *several*
several pronounced *sev'ral*	= a *few*
several pronounced **sev**'ral	= a *fair few*
several pronounced *SEV'ral*	= *part a fair few*
several pronounced **SEV**'ral	= *best part a fair few*

The Monologue

These two wuds, *sev'ral* and *few*,
Depict th' Suff'k dialect, oh soo trew.
'At's th' oldest English tongue,
Stand'd English, is oh soo young.

These two wuds, *sev'ral* and *few*,
Depict the Suff'k dialect, oh soo trew.
Flexable and suttle, and soo aware,
Of what's around 'em, everywhere.

Accurately stayt'n ut, in wuds just a few,
Depict'n th' Suff'k dialect, oh soo trew.
Quoite opp'sit t' th' others who
Will use th' best part a fair few.

Th' Suff'k dialect must ne'er be dead,
'At's th' moost ancient English ever said.
'At must laarst fer **SEV**'ral years to come,
Else England t'gather – will talk as one.

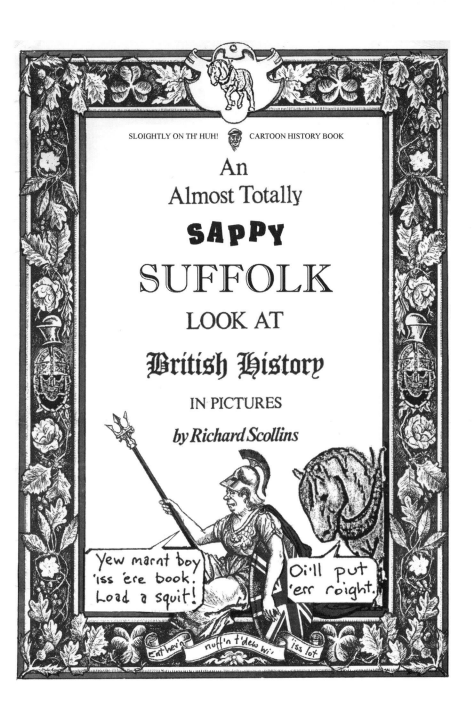

SLOIGHTLY ON TH' HUH!   CARTOON HISTORY BOOK

An
Almost Totally
SAPPY
SUFFOLK
LOOK AT
British History
IN PICTURES

by Richard Scollins

Yew marnt boy 'iss 'ere book. Load a squit!

Oi'll put 'err roight.

En'theys nuffin t'dew wi' 'iss lot

Alfred and the Cakes — 878

**Canute Demonstrates His Inability to
Turn the Tide — AD 1020**

Lady Godiva — 1057

The Battle of Hastings — 1066

The Death of William Rufus — 1100

King John and Magna Carta — 1215

**Edward I Presents His Son as
Prince of Wales — 1284**

Bruce and the Spider — 1306

The Battle of Agincourt — 1415

Richard III at Bosworth — 1485

Henry VIII and Anne Boleyn — 1529

Raleigh and the Puddle — 1581

Francis Drake Goes Bowling — 1588

The First Night of 'Hamlet' — 1601

The Gunpowder Plot — 1605

The Execution of Charles I — 1649

**Charles II and Friends Hide From
the Roundheads — 1651**

Isaac Newton Discovers Gravity — 1666

**Bonnie Prince Charlie Arrives
in Scotland — 1745**

Nelson at Trafalgar — 1805

Wellington Inspects His Troops — 1815

The Charge of the Light Brigade — 1854

Stanley Greets Dr. Livingstone — 1871

Queen Victoria 'Not Amused' — 1878

TH' END

£3 Special Offer!

Buying this book can **SAVE** you £3, when you order

one of Charlie Haylock's CDs of East Anglian mardles and monologues.

"That's Jest Cost Yew a Beer" or "A Pint o' Adnams Best" each retail at £13 incl. p&p.

BUT ONLY £10 <u>each</u> when you order direct, quoting reference "On Th' Huh!"

Write with full name and address to:-
ON TH' HUH CD OFFER
8 Minsmere Way
Gt Cornard, Sudbury
Suffolk CO10 OLB
cheques payable to **CHARLIE HAYLOCK**
or phone 01787-311736 to book Charlie for after dinner speaking.